SMILE

NOW

You May Not Feel Like It Latter

SCOTT BRECKHEIMER

Glendale Heights, IL 60139

Compiled by Scott Breckheimer

Cover Design by Design Dynamics
Illustrations by Pete Secker

Published by Great Quotations, Inc.

Library of Congress Catalog Card Number : 98-075784

ISBN: 1-56245-375-0

Printed in Hong Kong

"In spite of the cost of living it's still popular."

Kathleen Norris

"I got the bill for my surgery. Now I know why those doctors were wearing masks."

James H. Barrie

"Better to remain silent and be thought a fool than to speak out and remove all doubt."

Abraham Lincoln

"A banker is a fellow who lends you his umbrella when the sun is shining and wants it back the minute it begins to rain."

"If you pick up a starving dog and make him prosperous, he will not bite you.

This is the principal difference between a dog and a man."

Mark Twain

"God must love the common man, he made so many of them."

Abraham Lincoln

"Retirement is when a man who figured he'd go fishing seven times a week finds himself washing the dishes three times a day."

"When a man steals your wife, there is no better revenge than to let him keep her."

Sacha Guitry

"If I had known I was going to live this long I would have taken better care of myself."

"There is nothing so annoying as to have two people go right on talking when you're interrupting."

Mark Twain

"If you want to know how many friends you have, just buy a cottage on a lake."

"It is better to give than to lend, and it costs about the same."

Sir Philip Gibbs

"We can't all be heroes because somebody has to sit on the curb and clap as they go by."

Will Rogers

"I drink to make other people more interesting."

George Jean Nathan

"It's not whether you win or lose– it's how you place the blame."

"**M**iracles are great, but they are so damned unpredictable."

Peter Drucker

"The drive-in bank was established so that the real owner of a car could get to see it once in a while."

"Let us be thankful for the fools. But for them the rest of us could not succeed."

Mark Twain

"Middle age is the time in life when it takes you longer to rest than it does to get tired."

"The brain is a wonderful organ; it starts the minute you get up in the morning and does not stop until you get to the office."

Robert Frost

"Guests,
like fish,
begin to
smell after
three days."

Benjamin Franklin

"Don't be humble: you're not that great."

Golda Meir

"Anyone can win, unless there happens to be a second entry."

George Ade

"You can always tell a real friend; when you've made a fool of yourself he doesn't feel you've done a permanent job."

Lawrence J. Peter

"Always borrow from a pessimist– he never expects it back."

"Even if you're on the right track, you'll get run over if you just sit there."

Will Rogers

"**B**lessed are the young, for they shall inherit the national debt."

"Advertising may be described as the science of arresting human intelligence long enough to get money from it."

"The closest to perfection a person ever comes is when they fill out a job application."

Stanley J. Randall

"**B**efore you borrow money from a friend, decide which you need more."

"The person who marries for money usually earns every penny of it."

"**H**appiness is a positive cash flow."

Fred Adler

"A jury should decide a case the minute they are shown it, before the lawyers have had a chance to mislead 'em."

Will Rogers

"Laugh and the world laughs with you, snore and you sleep alone."

Anthony Burgess

"Love is the answer;
but while you are
waiting for the answer,
sex raises some pretty
good questions."

Woody Allen

"If at first you don't succeed, try, try again…then give up. There's no use being a damn fool about it."

W.C. Fields

"Some who are not paid what they are worth ought to be glad."

"When I was a boy of fourteen, my father was so ignorant I could hardly stand to have the old man around. But when I got to be twenty-one I was astonished at how much the old man had learned in seven years."

Mark Twain

"Three may keep a secret, if two of them are dead."

Benjamin Franklin

"**A** chip on the shoulder is often a piece of wood that has fallen from the head."

"The two hardest things to handle in life are failure and success."

"Ninety-eight percent of the adults in this country are decent, hard-working, honest Americans. It's the other lousy two percent that get all the publicity. But then we elected them."

Lily Tomlin

"Some people are like a callus; they always show up when the work is finished."

"**M**oney won't buy happiness, but it will pay the salaries of a large research staff to study the problem."

Bill Vaughan

"Only two groups of people fall for flattery–men and women."

"A nickel goes a long way now. You can carry it around for days without finding a thing it will buy."

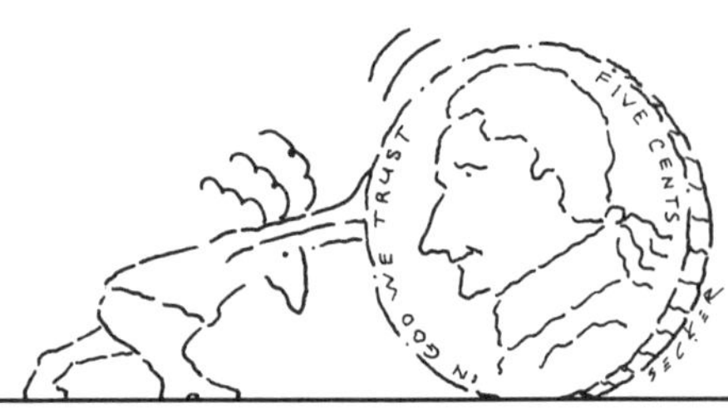

"Suppose you were an idiot and suppose you were a member of Congress. But I repeat myself."

Mark Twain

"When opportunity knocks, some people are in the backyard looking for four-leaf clovers."

"All you need to grow fine, vigorous grass is a crack in your sidewalk."

Will Rogers

"Diplomacy:

Thinking twice before saying nothing."

"A man can't be too careful in the choice of his enemies."

Oscar Wilde

"I don't make jokes. I just watch the government and report the facts."

Will Rogers

"All husbands are alike, but they have different faces so you can tell them apart."

Anonymous

"Always forgive your enemies– nothing annoys them so much."

Oscar Wilde

"If you get up early,
work late, and
pay your taxes, you
will get ahead–
if you win the lotto!"

"Lead your life so you wouldn't be ashamed to sell the family parrot to the town gossip."

"The only fool bigger than the person who knows it all is the person who argues with him."

"It is ill-mannered to silence a fool, and cruelty to let him go on."

Benjamin Franklin

"I've had a wonderful evening," said Groucho Marx after a very dull party, "but this wasn't it."

"If all the economists in the world were laid end to end, it would probably be a good thing."

"When the
well's dry,
we know the
worth of water."

"**H**e that
scatters thorns,
let him not
go barefoot."

"**O**ne nice thing about egotists:

They don't talk about other people."

"Love your enemies, for they tell you your faults."

"Income tax has made more liars out of the American people than golf has."

Will Rogers

"You have only to mumble a few words in church to get married and a few words in your sleep to get divorced."

"After all is said and done, more is said than done."

"I don't jog. If I die, I want to be sick."

Abe Lemons

"There are two times when a man doesn't understand a woman– before marriage and after marriage."

"If you tell the truth, you don't have to remember anything."

Mark Twain

"When you have got an elephant by the hind legs and he is trying to run away, it is best to let him run."

Abraham Lincoln

"Some people don't have much to say, but you have to listen a long time to find it out."

"Forgive your enemies, but never forget their names."

John F. Kennedy

"Vacation–
The period when
those rainy days
for which a
person saves,
usually arrive."

"**A** jury consists of twelve persons chosen to decide who has the better lawyer."

Robert Frost

Murphy's law:

"If anything can go wrong, it will."

O'Toole's commentary on Murphy's law:

"Murphy was an optimist."

Other Titles by Great Quotations, Inc.

Hard Covers

Ancient Echoes
Behold the Golfer
Commanders in Chief
The Essence of Music
First Ladies
Good Lies for Ladies
Great Quotes From Great Teachers
Great Women
I Thought of You Today
Journey to Success
Just Between Friends
Lasting Impressions
My Husband My Love
Never Ever Give Up
The Passion of Chocolate
Peace Be With You
The Perfect Brew
The Power of Inspiration
Sharing the Season
Teddy Bears
There's No Place Like Home

Paperbacks

301 Ways to Stay Young
ABC's of Parenting
Angel-grams
African American Wisdom
Astrology for Cats
Astrology for Dogs
The Be-Attitudes
Birthday Astrologer
Can We Talk
Chocoholic Reasonettes
Cornerstones of Success
Daddy & Me
Erasing My Sanity
Graduation is Just the Beginning
Grandma I Love You
Happiness is Found Along the Wa
Hooked on Golf
Ignorance is Bliss
In Celebration of Women
Inspirations
Interior Design for Idiots

Great Quotations, Inc.
1967 Quincy Court
Glendale Heights,IL 60139 USA
Phone: 630 582-2800 Fax: 630-582-2813
http://www.greatquotations.com

Other Titles by Great Quotations, Inc.

Paperbacks

I'm Not Over the Hill
Life's Lessons
Looking for Mr. Right
Midwest Wisdom
Mommy & Me
Mother, I Love You
The Mother Load
Motivating Quotes
Mrs.Murphy's Laws
Mrs. Webster's Dictionary
Only A Sister
The Other Species
Parenting 101
Pink Power
Romantic Rhapsody
The Secret Langauge of Men
The Secret Langauge of Women
The Secrets in Your Name
A Servant's Heart
Social Disgraces
Stress or Sanity
A Teacher is Better Than
Teenage of Insanity
Touch of Friendship
Wedding Wonders
Words From the Coach

Perpetual Calendars

365 Reasons to Eat Chocolate
Always Remember Who Loves You
Best Friends
Coffee Breaks
The Dog Ate My Car Keys
Extraordinary Women
Foundations of Leadership
Generations
The Heart That Loves
The Honey Jar
I Think My Teacher Sleeps at Schoo
I'm a Little Stressed
Keys to Success
Kid Stuff
Never Never Give Up
Older Than Dirt
Secrets of a Successful Mom
Shopoholic
Sweet Dreams
Teacher Zone
Tee Times
A Touch of Kindness
Apple a Day
Golf Forever
Quotes From Great Women
Teacher Are First Class